BUCK O'NEIL:
A Baseball Legend

BUCK O'NEIL: A Baseball Legend

by Sean D. Wheelock

International Standard Book Number 0-8488-1687-0 (hardcover)
International Standard Book Number 0-8488-1688-9 (softcover)

Manufactured in the United States of America

for my mom, Judy
with love

TABLE OF CONTENTS

Baseball *fulfilled me like music. I played most of my life and I loved it. Waste no tears for me. I wasn't born too early. I was right on time.*
>   *—Buck O'Neil, Kansas City Monarchs*

In 1950 former player Hallie Harding, then the sports editor of the *Los Angeles Sentinel*, wrote a story in which he maligned Negro baseball. Buck O'Neil's response was, "There are approximately two hundred men in the Negro league now. They earn from $200 to $800 monthly for five months. Some eighty-odd of these will draw this amount from winter league baseball. These salaries, of course, will not compare to those of [Ted] Williams or [Joe] DiMaggio with their multi-thousand dollar draws. But it beats the hell out of loafing on Beale Street [in Memphis] or Eighteenth and Vine [in Kansas City].

INTRODUCTION

He took me back. I don't know that he was trying to take me, and I don't know that I was expecting to go. Yet, sitting with him that afternoon, time became meaningless. The day, the month, the year, outside of that room, that door, no longer mattered. For inside, it was his time, and I found myself with him. His face grew more expressive now, his eyes brighter, his voice more commanding. It seemed to be the present that he spoke of, not the very long ago past. Memories that might have faded, were now back in vivid and brilliant clarity. Details that were feared lost, had returned with startling accuracy. This bygone era he now spoke of was brought right before me. I could feel it, I could share it with him. This was his time all right, and for those fleeting moments it was mine too. He talked of Satchel Paige now, and Cool Papa Bell. Of Josh Gibson, Hilton Smith, Buck Leonard. He told me about Jackie Robinson and Ernie Banks. The Homestead Grays, the New York Black Yankees, the Pittsburgh Crawfords, the Kansas City Monarchs. Chicago, Newark, Birmingham, Des Moines, Sioux City, Memphis, Baltimore, St. Joe. The segregated restaurants, the long bus rides, the winters in Latin America, the sold out stadiums. It was the feel of the time of which he spoke, the frenetic excitement of knowing that what you are doing is something very special, never to be repeated or relived. The picture he painted with his words was full of robust and vibrant color. There was no bitterness in this voice, only joy and satisfaction. He had lived in a time that was now long gone, never to be seen again. And while he was there, Buck O'Neil made it his own. He took me back that afternoon, back with him.

BUCK O'NEIL:

We were very famous, we really were. It was an exciting time, it really was. Those were exciting times see because actually, jazz was running high. And Kansas City was right in the middle of it. And black baseball was running high. And the Kansas City Monarchs was right in the middle of it. And it was so alive, and a whole lot of things were happening around here. And we were a part of every aspect in the community. The church, it's like now. We had an 11:00 service. We go to church from 11:00 to 1:00. When the Monarchs were playing we went to church from 10:00 to 12:00 so they could get out and come see the Monarchs. Just like that. The preacher would have a sermon and invite us all. Baseball sermon. All these things happening There was so many things happening and all about 18th and Vine and 12th Street. The restaurants, the drugstores, everything was alive when the Monarchs was in town. People were com-

ing, they would just congregate. Talk to the Monarchs and see the Monarchs. And they knew us and we knew them. And ball clubs would come to town and come in here. They would come Saturday and be on around 18th and Vine and 12th Street and all that neighborhood on Saturday, and eating at the restaurants, different things. People just like this. And we'd talk to the people. Rube Foster would come on that corner, 18th and Vine, and stand out on that corner. There was a Crown Drugstore on the corner at that time. And he would stand on that corner and talk about what he was going to do to the Monarchs that Sunday. And that Saturday night, maybe a Basie would be playing in the subway. Or Charlie Parker would be blowing somewhere, and we knew all these people. Now in the ball game, all these people coming to the ball park. They're coming to the ball park. The Ella Fitzgeralds and all them, they're going to see us play ball. Oh, we had a wonderful time, but guys in the neighborhood, they had a good time too. Because it was different then, for them even. You know what I mean.

CHAPTER 1

BUCK O'NEIL:

The Kansas City Monarchs played straight baseball. The House of David, they wore beards and did shadow games and things like that. The team in our league was the Indianapolis Clowns. They got in the league later, in the 40's, and they would put on shows before the ball game. And the people liked it, really enjoyed it. Because they were actually funny. And because on that club was Goose Tatum. Did you ever see Goose Tatum on the basketball court with the Harlem Globetrotters? Well he was as funny as anybody you've ever seen. He was a baseball player too. And those antics he would play

*on the baseball field. Ah man, the
people really liked it. I liked it. You
know what I mean, I enjoyed seeing
it when they put the show on. You
see, the Clowns would do all these
acts, but they expected us to beat
them, and we did. With the Monarchs, you thought baseball. That's
all you thought.*

He knew he wanted to manage. As a boy
in Jim Crow Florida of the 1920's, Buck
O'Neil became transfixed by baseball. Although he could not sit with the white fans, he
could watch the white teams going through
their spirited training paces, from the segregated "colored" section. And he could also
see the black teams, and in these games Buck
O'Neil saw his future.

Buck O'Neil:

*I always wanted to manage. You
know a lot of people asked me, way
back when I was a kid, who was
your favorite baseball player, things*

like that. At the time, in Sarasota, the Giants trained there. John McGraw was managing the ball club. Down in Fort Myers, 70 miles from us, the Athletics were down there, Connie Mack. What fascinated me more than the ball players—the managers. Connie Mack would manage and he'd have a suit on, a hat and all. And he's sitting in the dugout with these flags and the score cards, and he's making all kinds of signs. Fascinated me.

And I was fortunate enough to have seen black baseball players. Not only the local black baseball players, I saw the black major league baseball players. Rube Foster would bring the Chicago American Giants to West Palm Beach for the winter, and C.I. Taylor would bring the Indianapolis ABC's to West Palm Beach for the winter. One of them represented The Breakers Hotel, which was a big resort hotel. The other one was The Royal Ponciana. And they played ball Thursdays and Sundays just to entertain the guests at the hotel. During that time, golf wasn't as popular, and tennis wasn't as popular. Football and basketball wasn't as popular. So everybody on Thursday afternoon and Sunday afternoon, everybody that worked in West Palm Beach, all on that beach, the maids, the butlers, the chauffeurs, all of them would come to the ball park, as well as the guests in the hotel. So, it was actually that all people would do this on Thursdays and Sundays. And my uncle took me down there to see that. See, I had been reading the paper, The Pittsburgh Courier, *the* Chicago Defendant. *See we got these papers,* The Amsterdam News, *and my daddy would get them so I could read these things about the games. And so I read about them, but I always wanted to see them. And you know,*

I saw the white ball players too. Yeah, I saw the Ruths, the Cobbs, and all them back there. But I'd never seen the black ball players I read about. And finally I went down there and I saw them. We went to see them one Thursday, and my uncle kept me down there so I saw them on Sunday too. And I knew what I wanted. Because I'd seen these guys play. I said, well hell, these guys just as good as those other guys.

John "Buck" O'Neil was born November 13, 1911, in Carrabelle, Florida. In 1924, he moved with his family to Sarasota, Florida, a town in which he first played organized baseball as a boy. The team was called the Sarasota Tigers, and although it was for high school aged boys, O'Neil was starting at first base while still in grammar school. He would continue to be a first basemen at Edward Waters College in Jacksonville, and then for the semi-pro Miami Giants.

It was with the Miami Giants that Buck

with the Harlem Globetrotters? Well he was as funny as anybody you've ever seen. He was a baseball player too. And those antics he would play on the baseball field. Ah man, the people really liked it. I liked it. You know what I mean, I enjoyed seeing it when they put the show on. You see, the Clowns would do all these acts, but they expected us to beat them, and we did. With the Monarchs, you thought baseball. That's all you thought.

He knew he wanted to manage. As a boy in Jim Crow Florida of the 1920's, Buck O'Neil became transfixed by baseball. Although he could not sit with the white fans, he could watch the white teams going through their spirited training paces, from the segregated "colored" section. And he could also see the black teams, and in these games Buck O'Neil saw his future.

Buck O'Neil:

I always wanted to manage. You know a lot of people asked me, way back when I was a kid, who was your favorite baseball player, things like that. At the time, in Sarasota, the Giants trained there. John McGraw was managing the ball club. Down in Fort Myers, 70 miles from us, the Athletics were down there, Connie Mack. What fascinated me more than the ball players—the managers. Connie Mack would manage and he'd have a suit on, a hat and all. And he's sitting in the dugout with these flags and the score cards, and he's making all kinds of signs. Fascinated me.

And I was fortunate enough to have seen black baseball players. Not only the local black baseball players, I saw the black major league baseball players. Rube Foster would bring the Chicago American Giants to West Palm Beach for the winter, and C.I. Taylor would bring the Indianapolis ABC's to West Palm Beach for the winter. One of them represented The Breakers Hotel, which was a big resort hotel. The other one was The Royal Ponciana. And they played ball Thursdays and Sundays just to entertain the guests at the hotel. During that time, golf wasn't as popular, and tennis wasn't as popular. Football and basketball wasn't as popular. So everybody on Thursday afternoon and Sunday afternoon, everybody that worked in West Palm Beach, all on that beach, the maids, the butlers, the chauffeurs, all of them would come to the ball park, as well as the guests in the hotel. So, it was actually that all people would do this on Thursdays and Sundays. And my uncle took me down there to see that. See, I had been reading the paper, The

Pittsburgh Courier, *the* Chicago Defendant. *See we got these papers,* The Amsterdam News, *and my daddy would get them so I could read these things about the games. And so I read about them, but I always wanted to see them. And you know, I saw the white ball players too. Yeah, I saw the Ruths, the Cobbs, and all them back there. But I'd never seen the black ball players I read about. And finally I went down there and I saw them. We went to see them one Thursday, and my uncle kept me down there so I saw them on Sunday too. And I knew what I wanted. Because I'd seen these guys play. I said, well hell, these guys just as good as those other guys.*

John "Buck" O'Neil was born November 13, 1911, in Carrabelle, Florida. In 1924, he moved with his family to Sarasota, Florida, a town in which he first played organized baseball as a boy. The team was called the Sarasota Tigers, and although it was for high school aged boys, O'Neil was starting at first base while still in grammar school. He would continue to be a first basemen at Edward Waters College in Jacksonville, and then for the semi-pro Miami Giants.

It was with the Miami Giants that Buck O'Neil first began to realize that baseball would not only be his passion, it would be his career.

In 1935, the ball club changed its name to the New York Tigers, and began to barnstorm around the country extensively. While on tour through Louisiana, the owner of the Shreveport Acme Giants, Winfield Welch, recognized the talent that Buck O'Neil possessed, and offered him a contract for the following season. The Acme Giants essentially served as a farm club for the Kansas City Monarchs of the Negro American League, and thus trained alongside the club in Shreveport during the spring. Following the 1936 season with the Acme Giants, Monarch owner J.L. Wilkinson purchased the contract of Buck O'Neil with the intention of making him the club's first basemen. With no room on the Monarchs however, O'Neil was sent to the Memphis Red Sox for the 1937 season. In 1938, Buck O'Neil became a Kansas City Monarch, a team for which he is most readily and prominently associated. He remained a Monarch through the 1955 season, when the team was sold, and left Kansas City.

From their inception in 1920, through the end of the 1955 season, the Kansas City Monarchs were the premiere organization in Negro league baseball. Although detailed records and statistics were not kept, decisions against non-black teams were generally lost, decisions against fellow Negro league teams were incomplete, it is clear that the Monarchs were one of the outstanding teams in all of baseball. This fact is established as such, based upon the ball clubs roster of players, their consistency in drawing huge crowds throughout North America, and their documented results against major league all-star teams.

Buck O'Neil:

See the Monarchs remind me so much of the New York Yankees. The Yankees, when they would come to St. Louis to play the Browns, pack the ball park. You understand what I mean. The man could pay his salaries, pay all his bills. The Yankees are coming to town, don't worry. When the Yankees come, we can pay off all these bills. That was the same thing with the Monarchs. When the franchise had a little problem, don't worry, the Monarchs and Satchel Paige is coming to town. And when we came to town, boom! Everybody's coming.

Throughout their history, the Kansas City Monarchs had many of the top stars in the Negro leagues, some of whom went on to be stars in the major leagues as well, once the color barrier was broken. Satchel Paige, Jackie Robinson, Ernie Banks, Chet Brewer, Bullet

Rogan, Elston Howard, Connie Johnson, Quincy Trouppe, and of course Buck O'Neil were just some of the notable players to have represented the Monarchs. Of all of these men however, it was Leroy "Satchel" Paige, who served as the ball club's main attraction.

Buck O'Neil:

He just might have been the greatest pitcher who ever lived. This is the sad part about it, that he couldn't pitch in the major leagues when he was young. Because I do believe that he would have rewritten the record book, because he was just that good.

Satchel had an outstanding fast ball, one of the best fast balls I've ever seen. And the best control I've ever seen. The best change of speeds I've ever seen. Wasn't a great curve ball pitcher, but he changed speeds on everything. He changed speeds on everything, and threw strikes with it. Not only strikes, he threw it where he wanted to throw it. It's different than just throwing a strike, but you throw strikes to different parts of the plate to the different hitters. And that's what he could do, that very few people could do.

You know, after we started billing Satchel Paige as the attraction, that's when Satchel started pitching one inning, two innings, three innings, just to make the appearance, see. This is why he pitched like that. Before that, Satchel would pitch nine innings just like anybody else.

Of the many legendary Satchel Paige exploits from his long and illustrious Hall of Fame career that persist, one of the more famous was when Paige actually called all of his fielders off of the playing field, leaving just himself, his catcher, and the hitter.

Buck O'Neil:

That had happened, but it happened actually because more or less he wanted to prove a point. Because some guy had said some things that he didn't like, and he just wanted to prove just how much better we were than they were. And that's why he called them in. He didn't want to just strike the side out. Now that wasn't a Major League ball club. No athlete would try to show up another athlete. You know what I mean, in the major leagues everybody out there was making a living. But this was actually a team that we played, and they had some people on it that was a little snotty. He just proved to them that, "ah man, you can't play."

Satchel was always a team player. But as I told a lot of people before, Satchel played on a team that I managed. Nobody managed Satchel.

At the premiere level of black baseball, the teams were grouped into the Negro American League, and the Negro National League. Scheduling however, was neither balanced nor consistent, with teams often changing cities and ownership from season to season. In 1940, for instance, the Kansas City Monarchs won the first half of the Negro American League season, victorious in 12 of 19 games. The Chicago American Giants meanwhile, played a total of 24 league games, the Indianapolis Crawfords, just 8. The second half standings were never published, yet the Monarchs were declared champions with an unknown record. For those who choose to judge greatness of individuals and teams based solely on statistics and won/loss records, the Negro league ball clubs and their players can never fully be appreciated or even understood. What the teams did was play baseball, a lot of it, throughout the year. Against other black major league teams, against local town teams, against semi-pro, college, and novelty teams. Even in the off season, playing against major league all-star teams, consisting of the top players from white baseball. The lifeblood of black baseball, quite simply, was barnstorming. Traveling the country, playing any and all challengers, in ball parks from

Yankee Stadium to high school fields in Iowa. Allowing all fans, white and black, to see baseball at a level that was nearly indistinguishable on the field from that of their Major League counterparts.

Buck O'Neil:

What we did in the schedule, was a lot of times, we played in these different towns with a league team. We would play two, maybe three days, because we would be playing in all these other towns. We would take the team in our territory, which was like St. Joe [Missouri], Topeka, Omaha, Des Moines. We would take them around.

Let's say we would bring the Chicago American Giants here, and we would play in Kansas City on Friday night. And we usually had off on Saturday, and then Sunday, a double-header here. And then maybe Monday, we would take them to St.

Joe. The next night, Tuesday, we would take them to Omaha. The next night, Wednesday, Des Moines. And after we finished that week with them, then we'd pick up another team here in Kansas City. Say we would pick up the Memphis Red Sox, and we would bring them in. Instead of taking them that route, we would take them maybe to Wichita, Oklahoma City, Tulsa, Springfield, Missouri. That was also our area. Then maybe the next week, we were going to Memphis to play. So Memphis, on the way maybe Friday night, Memphis would take us into Little Rock. Then Little Rock, and on the weekend, we're going to play a ball game on Saturday night in Memphis, and a double-header Sunday in Memphis. Then Monday, probably, Greenville, Mississippi. Tuesday, Jackson, Mississippi. This is the way we played them, see. So we got around quite a bit.

All of these are league games, but we would play them in different towns. See, what we had was a split season, and whoever won the first half would play the team that won the second half. This would be for the league championship. And then, they would do the same thing in the East, which was the Negro National League. And we would play the championship out there. That's the way we played our World Series.

But, you know, I also played on some small fields, too. Actually, I played in some fields where we would lay fields out ourselves. More or less, we played a lot of fair dates in the autumn of the year around Kansas and Missouri, and lots of places where we didn't actually have a diamond, so we made the diamonds and played. And the Monarchs would bring in the lights, and after the game, that was an

*attraction itself. People would come
to see the lights and see a ball game.*

Of the many things that are misconstrued
and misunderstood about black baseball, one
that remains prominent is the way in which
the teams traveled around the country. While
it may be believed through films such as the
1976 release "Bingo Long Traveling All-Stars
and Motor Kings," that conditions on the road
were horrific, quite the opposite was generally the case. These players were icons in the
black community, and certainly celebrities to
the residents, both black and white, in the
towns and cities to which they traveled.

Buck O'Neil:

*One thing about it is, in the city,
we stayed in the best black hotels. We
ate at the best restaurants, but they
just happened to be black. But some-
times, you would go to the small
towns and with us mostly, we stayed
in peoples' homes. And one thing*

about it is, we stayed in the best homes, because we stayed in maybe the preacher's home. Maybe someone else would stay in the undertaker's home. Some of us would stay in the principal's home. This was the way it was. That was the towns that didn't have the hotels. But most all the teams in the leagues, you know, they had hotels that could accommodate you.

Most of the traveling was, say you played Chicago, then you played in Gary [Indiana], you played South Bend [Indiana]. You stayed right in Chicago. You understand what I'm saying. And you go out there to South Bend, 90 miles, then Gary, 30 miles. So these are the things that happen, and the big travel was maybe we would go every year, we would go east. The teams from the west would go east to play, and we would play those teams out there. Like in New York City, we would play the New York Black Yankees and the Memphis Red Sox would play the New York Cubans in a double-header at Yankee Stadium. They drew well and the same thing could happen at Ebbets Field, and this is the way it happened. But getting there was your longest jump. We'd play our way out there, maybe we'd leave Chicago, then we'd play in Columbus, Ohio. Maybe then we'd play Cincinnati, Columbus, Pittsburgh. Now we got to go over the mountains to get to wherever, Philadelphia, wherever we were going, New York or Newark. So those were actually the longest jumps. Now occasionally we would have to make a long jump. I remember once we came from New York to Kansas City. It's two days. We play that Thursday in Yankee Stadium, and we had to play here [Kansas City] Sunday. That was a long jump, and that didn't happen too often. Because usually the way the games were scheduled, you didn't have to make the long jumps. The thing that you heard, that they slept in the bus, well that wasn't the Monarchs, it wasn't a team in the Negro American or Negro National League. A lot of people slept in the bus, because there's a lot of teams touring over the country. And those type ball clubs, they weren't in the league.

While black ball players were not accepted into Major League baseball prior to 1947, they were accepted by white fans throughout the country, when on the baseball diamond. Like their sports contemporaries, Joe Louis and Jesse Owens, sports fans recognized that these men were superb athletes, and thus received and appreciated accordingly. It was at the ball park when a Negro league team played, that all fans could cheer the excellence that was presented before them.

Buck O'Neil:

White people came out when we played white independent teams, and when we played our league teams. Just say if we played a team in Omaha, it just could have been fifty-fifty. If we would take a team to Sioux City [Iowa], it would be more white than black, because there wasn't that many blacks. And all over, it all depended on the places we played. Just like, we played in St. Joe, and actually we had a bigger white crowd than black, because there were more white people in St. Joe. And when we played in St. Joe, everybody came to the ball park, because they wanted to see the Monarchs, you know, white, black, anybody. The really true fans would come to see us play. They came. We drew crowds, wonderful crowds. And this is why we drew, because of the special occasion like thing. Well it was a holiday when the Monarchs were in town, because all the people from the surrounding towns would come in to see the Monarchs play.

With the major leagues, the fact was that there was radio at the time. So, you could read about it in the paper, and you'd hear the game on radio. But you didn't get a chance to see a Major League ball player. Here, you'd have to go to Chicago. You'd have to go to a Major League city to see a Major League baseball player. Wherein, when we started barnstorming, we would go to these cities that didn't have a chance to see baseball, and so we'd pack the ball park. It was really like a holiday. When just say, we would take a ball club like the Chicago American Giants to Sioux City, Iowa to play, few black people. But all the people in town would come to see, because they wanted to see this type of base-

ball that we were playing. And we did it all over.

We'd get better coverage in a small town, than say in Kansas City. Because see, in the small towns this was an occasion. So it would be in the local papers. And the people liked us to come to town, the merchants. With the Monarchs there, the restaurants, the hotels, everybody going to make some money.

Aside perhaps from the World Series, the most compelling and talent laden baseball games of the year would actually occur during the off season. Stars from the major leagues would form all-star teams, and barnstorm the country with their Negro league counterparts. These series of games not only brought the top black and white players in baseball to thousands of fans who otherwise would have had no opportunity to see them, it enabled the black players to prove that they could compete on a Major League level.

Buck O'Neil:

These games happened before my time, and during my time. When we would play the Major League ball clubs, ah man, you'd have to open the gates an hour before time. People just coming in like that.

See, I played, well the Monarchs, we played the Dizzy Dean All-Stars before the war. And after the war, we played the Bob Feller All-Stars. We'd play them all over. The guys in the east would play the Lefty Grove All-Stars. Every year somebody would get a ball club, because this was a good way to make a lot of money. And I'm sure, a lot of guys that played with the Bob Feller All-Stars probably made more money in that month than maybe they made all year.

It was all very friendly. We usually won, and one of the things about it is we were good athletes, so were they. But I think we had a little more to prove than they did. You know, they were reputed to be the best because that was the major leagues. We wanted to let everybody know that we were as good as anybody. And this is why I think we put a little more in it than they did.

For Buck O'Neil, being a member of the Kansas City Monarchs meant being a prominent member of the community as well,—his community. Ball players from the Monarchs, the Negro American and the Negro National Leagues as a whole, were accessible heroes to their fans. They lived in the neighborhoods, ate at the restaurants, shopped at the stores, just as their supporters did. They could be cheered at the ball park, and yet remain approachable in the street. The visiting teams would stay in a hotel in these same neighborhoods, and from the marquee player, to the reserve, they were there, out amongst the people.

Buck O'Neil:

One thing about it is that at one time everybody lived in the city just about. Everything was right there, together. Everybody was right down here, and so that meant everybody knew everybody. And that meant, all those kids had a chance to know the Monarchs, they knew all of us. And when the teams came in, and their players, everybody down here knew them.

But the kid that's coming in here now, well he doesn't live down here. He's in the suburbs and things like that. So these kids don't get a chance to know them. And the ball players don't get a chance to know them. So the only place now you get to see a ball player, is at the ball park.

See with the Monarchs, down around 18th and Vine, oh man, everything was jumping when we had

*a game. It was outstanding, a really
good feeling.*

In the winter months, the players of the Negro leagues would continue to earn money, either by playing baseball in Mexico or Latin America, or working jobs away from the sport. While the salaries in the Negro American or National Leagues were considerably higher than those of most other job opportunities available to these men, they still had to be augmented by off-season income.

Buck O'Neil:

I went down to Mexico, went to Cuba. And so this was what the ball players did. The better ball players played darn near year–round. The guys that didn't go to the Latin countries, they'd get a job. It wasn't too hard because we were very popular. Because with me, I stopped going to Cuba, and when the season was over, I'd go to the post office. And the guy at the post office, he said to me, anytime you need a job Buck, anytime. When the season is over with, just let me know when you're coming." And so I'd go to the post office and work. If I hadn't stayed in baseball, I would have retired from the postal service.

One thing about it is, I don't envy the players now with the salaries, because I've seen Major League ball players come to the post office in the winter to work, because they didn't make enough money. There was a time, when I think the owners took advantage of them. You got some kind of bargaining power now that you didn't have before. Because before, if you weren't satisfied with the salary, that's all right, we won't pay you. You didn't have a job. And you couldn't go somewhere else, because that team controlled you.

During that time, the majority of guys that went into baseball had a high school education. Actually, the job he had in baseball, he made more money than anything he could do. That's white and black, they made more money in baseball. But he still had to earn a living during the winter. At one time we must have had as many as six college educated players on this ball club. And these guys would play ball in the summer, and go teach school in the winter. And then, we had some that actually couldn't read.

CHAPTER 2

Buck O'Neil:

I figured it was going to change, because other things were changing. When you look at Jesse Owens and Joe Louis, and other things were changing, you know. So eventually, it was going to change. And I didn't think it was going to be the white man's heart that made it change. The commercial aspect. This is a capitalistic society. So that makes sense.

On April 18, 1946, in Jersey City, New Jersey, Jackie Robinson opened the season as the starting second baseman for the Montreal Royals of the International League. A year later, Robinson would debut at first base for the Royals' parent club, the Brooklyn Dodgers, thus breaking Major League Baseball's color barrier. Neither the major leagues, nor the Negro leagues, nor the entire sport of baseball for that matter, would ever be the same again.

For Buck O'Neil, 1946 was, like for so many professional baseball players, black and white, a year of adjustment. A season that saw a return to the sport after time spent serving in World War II. O'Neil had missed the 1944 and 1945 baseball seasons, serving in the United States Navy. Ironically, it was during the 1945 season that Jackie Robinson played his only season in the Negro leagues. His team was the Kansas City Monarchs.

Buck O'Neil:

I went into the service in '44, I didn't know Jackie. I met Jackie in Cuba in that winter in '46. He had played with Montreal and the Dodgers played some ball games in Cuba. I was in Cuba, and so we played some ball games down there, and that's when I met Jackie and Rachel [Robinson, Jackie's wife]. Then later that season we were in New York. We were playing the New York Cubans, and we were going to play them that night at Yankee Stadium. And during the day we went out to Brooklyn to see the Dodgers play. That's when Pee Wee Reese, I had met Pee Wee before, and Eddie Stanky, came over to me. And I said, "Does Jackie got a chance?" And they'd say, "Yeah, he's got a chance. We're going to see that he gets a chance."

And you know, he took Stanky's job. But these guys, it was actually, they had sense enough to know that Jackie's going to raise the salary of every ball player that played.

The success of Jackie Robinson as a member of the Brooklyn Dodgers was realized immediately in his first Major League season. Robinson batted .297, scored 125 runs, stole a league leading 29 bases, and was named baseball's Rookie of the Year. Perhaps even more important to the Dodgers' management, he enticed black fans to attend ball games at a rate never seen before in the team's, or the league's history. Any person who may have stayed away because Jackie Robinson was a member of the Brooklyn Dodgers, was soon forgotten, because so many more were attending games to see this great player. This was true in Brooklyn, as it was throughout the cities of the National League, in which the Dodgers played.

Buck O'Neil:

What forced the National League to bring in black players, was the Dodgers and the Giants. Right there in New York. Bill Veeck was over there in Cleveland. They started get-

Buck O'Neil and William Dismukes. In 1911, Dizzy Dismukes pitched three games in two days for the Indianapolis ABCs, winning them all including one that lasted twelve innings.

The Kansas City Monarchs, 1940. Seated, left to right: Floyd Kransen, Lionel DeCuir, Henry Milton, Junius (Rainey) Bibbs, Newt Allen, Hilton Smith, Dick Bradley. Standing: Quincy Gilmore (business manager), Andy Cooper, Joe Greene, Jesse Williams, Norman (Turkey) Stearnes, Jack Matchett, Leandy Young, John (Buck) O'Neil.

Left to right, Satchel Paige, Joe Greene and Hilton Smith in 1941. Hilton Smith was one of the all-time great pitchers.

The Kansas City Monarchs, 1921. Top row, left to right: Rube Currie, John Donaldson, Frank Blattner, Sam Crawford, George Carr, Walter Moore, Middle row: Wilber (Bullet) Rogan, Bartolo Portuando, Zack Foreman, Hurley McNair, Lemuel Hawkins, Otto Ray. Front row: Sylvester Foreman, Robert Fagan. Both Ray and Hawkins were traded to the Chicago Giants for catcher Frank Duncan shortly after this photograph was taken.

The *1946 Negro Baseball Yearbook* with Jackie Robinson on the cover.
It was announced on October 23, 1945 that Robinson had signed a
contract to play for the Montreal Royals, the Brooklyn Dodgers Triple
A farm team, making Robinson the first black player in the twentieth
century to be under contract to a major league team.

ting black ball players, and so what happened was actually this. The Yankees would play at Yankee Stadium. It didn't worry them, because they were going to fill up their ball park anyway, with all white folks. But it would hurt another team. It would hurt the Giants, if the Giants were playing, and the Dodgers were playing, and all the black folks were going over to the Dodgers to see them. To see Jackie play. And nobody's coming to see the Giants play, that made a difference. So the Giants started getting a lot of black Cuban ball players. They got a lot of black ball players on the Giants ball team. Well the Yankees, the American League, was a little slow, see. Because actually, their thinking was this. This was holding up that white flag. We're sticking out for the white race. That's just the way they were thinking about it. And during that time, the best white ball player in *the country, wanted to play with the Yankees. Because the Yanks were popular, and there wasn't nothing on the Yanks but white. The Yanks was white, and this is why if a scout would go in to try to sign a white ball player for Brooklyn, and a scout would go in to try to sign that guy for the Yankees, the Yankees would walk out with that ball player. See, because you know what I mean. Going to tell daddy, going to tell his momma, well he's going with the Yankees, they got more white play-ers over there. So, that's the way it happened. That's the way it was until the other teams got so good. Now the other teams got so good, now I got to go get me some of these guys.*

The last team in Major League Baseball to integrate was the Boston Red Sox. It was not until the 1959 season, that Elijah "Pumpsie" Green became a member of the ball club, thus completing the full integration of the sport, some twelve years since Jackie Robinson first donned a Brooklyn Dodgers uniform, three years after Robinson's retirement from the game.

Buck O'Neil:

See, what the Red Sox thought was actually, we don't need it, because we're in a position to get the best white ball player out there. And we don't need it here in Boston. See, because in Boston, you didn't have a Harlem. That made the difference. So, now what you're thinking is now I got to compete. So I got to get the best ball player, and I don't give a damn what he is.

In 1943, a year that began to see the top ball players leave the sport for military service in World War II, Bill Veeck made the Major League Baseball owners, and the game's commissioner, Judge Kenesaw Mountain Landis, a most unique proposal. The twenty-nine year old Veeck, who would later gain notoriety and infamy as owner of the Cleveland Indians, St. Louis Browns, and Chicago White Sox, offered to buy the Philadelphia Phillies, a team that had finished either last or next to last in the National League for ten consecutive seasons, and stock them exclusively with star players from the Negro leagues. While Veeck went on to bring exploding scoreboards, uniforms with shorts, a midget, a one armed outfielder, and many other never before seen innovations to the game, he was quickly blocked in this would-be historic quest. The Phillies were instead sold to William Cox, and remained at or near the bottom of the league for the next five seasons. Veeck would however, be successful in his bid for the Cleveland Indians, where he went on to integrate the American League, bringing Larry Doby to the ball club late in the 1947 season.

Buck O'Neil:

I heard about it. All this and what he wanted to do. But that was going to do the same thing that had been done. Maybe you're going to put a black team in the major leagues. Well, it's all right to put a black team, if you had black players on every other team. It was just a case to whether it just happened to have been all the players on the team was black. But just to pick a black team to put in the major leagues, now you're right back to square one. They wouldn't let him do it, because it would have been segregation in a different form.

The issue of Bill Veeck and the proposed all-black Philadelphia Phillies, raised a pressing question to the forefront; can a black player compete with a white player on the Major League level? While the answer to this question may have been known to those in baseball all along, it was still a topic open to debate amongst the fans of the sport.

Buck O'Neil:

Yeah, we were just as good. The only thing about it, what we would have done with the Monarchs, we would have added some players, because where we had nineteen, the major leagues had twenty-five players. So we would have had to add some pitching, I'm sure. And the pitching, it was out there. The pitching staff we had here with Satchel Paige, Hilton Smith, Booker McDaniel. We had some guys that were outstanding pitchers here. So, we could have gotten guys like Verdel Mathis from the Memphis ball club, and Aug Cornelius from the Chicago American Giants, or Ted Trent from the St. Louis ball club. We could have had excellent teams, but actually, the way we played, we didn't need that many pitchers.

The question of ability was quickly answered due to the immediate success of

Jackie Robinson, and the other pioneer black Major League players, like Elston Howard, Willie Mays, Roy Campanella, Hank Aaron, Larry Doby, and Don Newcombe, to name just a few of the many. It wasn't long after the color barrier was broken in 1947, that things like the aforementioned ability, as well as desire, character, and heart, in black players were accepted as equal to those of their white counterparts. The issues ultimately became those of how will the fans react to these black players? How will their teammates, manager, coaches, general manager and owner act and react towards them? Will society in general take to the integration of the national pastime? Above all else, economics, even ahead of racism and the battle against it, was the deciding factor in the desegregation of baseball. An all white game simply was not as economically feasible as an integrated one. The fan base opened up, a new talent pool of players made for a superior on-field product, and ultimately, the Negro leagues, which had served as legitimate competition to Major League Baseball, were destroyed.

Buck O'Neil:

I've never had a problem being accepted by the white players, even long before Jackie, when we played the major league all-stars. I just wasn't accepted into the Major Leagues, but as a ball player, I was accepted by all the guys that played. I was accepted by the other ball players, because what they wanted to do was compete. Because if you say you're the best, you want to be sure that you're competing with the best. And this is the way that the Major League ball players felt. That they had heard of us, seen us play, and so they wanted to see just how good we were. And we could see that of them, playing against each other. But they wanted to match them with us, just to see how good they were. That's with any good athlete, no problem. The only problem probably would have been with say, the bench player, or the guy that wasn't that good. Now he knew this, that if I got a job playing Major League Baseball, he would lose his job. But Stan Musial didn't have that problem, because he knew he could play. And all the great ball players, the guys that could play, that didn't bother them any.

One thing about it is competition. The main thing was competition. In fighting, this was going on back before Jack Johnson. This was Jack Johnson. Joe Louis actually made the money. He put more people in the arena than anybody else, and he was a good fighter, so that made them go to that. And at that time you had a lot of good white fighters, but you don't have them anymore. Just every once in a while, they want to make him something, because if he can fight, he's going to make a lot of money, because he's white. The guy that made a film, the Rocky film. Now you didn't have a white guy

that could beat a black guy in box-
ing. No way. So you created a movie.
So what Rocky did, Rocky beat the
black champion. And so they still
play Rocky films, and people will go
see them.

As far as baseball, it goes back to
what I was telling you. See, they
only had sixteen teams in the major
leagues. And every town in the
United States had a baseball team.
All of the factories had a baseball
team. It's kind of like everywhere
you looked was talent. A baseball
team like the Dodgers, might have
twenty minor league ball clubs, and
all of these guys are playing ball,
trying to get to the major leagues.
Also the supply was greater than the
demand. That's right. And so, the
majority of the guys that was playing Major League Baseball, or
wanted to go into organized baseball, at that time, the majority of
baseball players came from high

school, not college. Because, one thing about it, the man that got his college education, he kind of looked down on baseball, as far as making a living. You understand what I mean. Because he went into some other field because there was a lot of fields open to him, if he's really intelligent. So you didn't get as many college guys. See, but college guys were playing baseball in college, actually for a scholarship. If you were in the Ivy League, you were just playing to be playing. You know, for the fun of it. Because being in the Ivy League in the first place, you had a good mind. So you're going to do something else with it. You're going to be a doctor or something. He wasn't even thinking about baseball. But here's a kid from South Carolina. He's in the textile mills. His daddy's been in there. Now he's got a chance to play ball. And now he's got a chance to get into orga-

nized baseball. Now, here comes the black guy. That's competition for him. So he didn't want this. See, that's the reason. You didn't want that because every time a black guy would play, that meant a white guy couldn't play. These kids wanted to play and be good ball players, but what happened, just like I said, if every time a black guy would play, then a white guy couldn't.

It is indisputable fact now, that Jackie Robinson was the right man to break baseball's color barrier. He possessed the talent, temperament, personality, and constitution to take on one of the most pivotal racial issues in American history. Robinson had the foresight to recognize that what he was undertaking, far surpassed the boundaries of the baseball diamond. And yet, it was as a baseball player that Robinson had to wage this historical battle.

At the time however, Jackie Robinson was not heralded, in fact, and even resented, for being chosen as the man to integrate the major leagues. Many of the top players of the Negro leagues felt that it should be them, and not Robinson, selected as the first black player in Major League Baseball. After all, Robinson was just 27 years of age, and had played only one season for the Kansas City Monarchs. It was argued in black baseball circles, that he hadn't paid his dues the way so many other players in the league had. There were certainly more talented players in the Negro leagues than Robinson, more experience, better known. Yet, it was Jackie Robinson, chosen by Branch Rickey and the Brooklyn Dodgers, to be baseball's racial pioneer.

Buck O'Neil:

They were thinking as a ball player, where I would have been thinking as a scholar. And Jackie was the most logical man he could have picked. Just think of Jackie's background, and the other guy's background. Because we had sev-

eral ball players at the time, they were better ball players than Jackie. Could have walked right into the major leagues and played. But these guys were thirty, thirty-five years old. And these guys didn't have the mentality really, to accept it, the things that Jackie did. Because Jackie knew that if he failed, it could be twenty years more, before this would have happened again. Because a lot of people in baseball resented that Branch Rickey signed Jackie. It could have set the picture back, where if some guy that was better than Jackie, had they come up, he'd probably gone and pulled the guy over who'd been heckling him, and smacked him so that would have been it. And they'd have said, I told you that's what they were going to do. But Jackie knew what it actually all meant. He was the perfect choice, and he could really play.

There were so many of them that didn't get a chance. And there were so many of them before Jackie. This is why they had the feelings that they felt. Because they knew there was better guys playing than Jackie.

Jackie Robinson not only opened up Major League Baseball to black players, he opened it up to Hispanics as well. While light skin Hispanic ball players were allowed into the major leagues prior to the integration of baseball, dark skin Hispanics were banned. Often, these men would play in the Negro leagues, spawning such team names as the New York Cubans and the Cuban X Giants.

Buck O'Neil:

Oh yeah, they played with us, and they played in the major leagues before we did. But it was the white Cubans. The white Cubans played in the major leagues, Adolfo Luque, and these guys, they played in the major leagues. And there was a lot of guys down there better than those guys, but you were just the wrong color. Like Luque, Luque's grandmother might have been black. It's just the way he's looking to them, you know, the people. He's got light skin. That's just what it was.

At one time, John McGraw had a light skin black guy. This guy had played with the American Giants. It was in the '20's. He was a good ball player, but when he came back to Chicago, those black fans came out to see him. John would have kept him, but the league wouldn't let him keep him.

For many years after integration of the major leagues in 1947, black players were not fully accepted as equal to their white teammates, in such places as hotels and restaurants. This continual racial discrimination existed far beyond the deep South, into every Major League city. Black players frequently

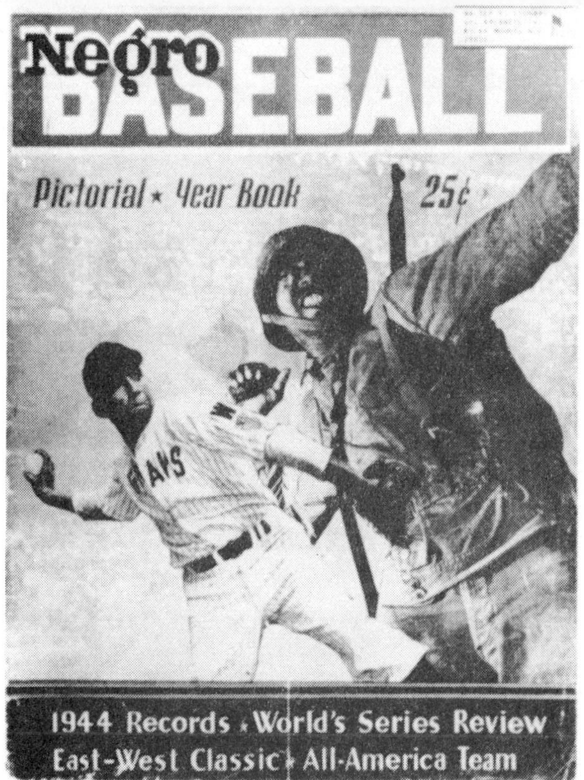

The *Negro Baseball Pictorial Year Book,* 1945. Making the throws are Buck Leonard (in baseball uniform) and an unidentified G.I. During World War II, more than fifty Negro league players served in the armed forces.

Comiskey Park on the day of the East-West Game, 1938.

Clockwise from top left, Spencer Williams and Tim Moore — stars of the "Amos 'n Andy Show", W. C. Handy, and Bessie Smith. Many entertainers were baseball fans and became close friends of the ball players.

Promoting night baseball, J. L: Wilkinson, owner of the Kansas City Monarchs, said "Night baseball will be to baseball what talkies were to movies." When the Monarchs began playing under lights in 1930, their attendance increased dramatically.

We have successfully lighted every kind of a ball park in the country, including both Major Leagues. AND CAN BELIGHT IN ALL OF THEM

Actual Photograph of One of the Many Towers Supporting the Flood Lights

Actual Photograph of Trucks Used to Transport the Monarch Lighting Plant and Towers

The Monarchs' bus burned on a Florida roadside after some clothing on board caught f
As the bus burned, Buck O'Neil, then, the manager, overheard a voice on the police ra
say, "Don't worry, it's just some niggers broke down."

Buck O'Neil. In 1962 he became the first black coach in the major
leagues when the Chicago Cubs signed him to work with their
infielders. Upon hearing the news, former Monarch owner Tom Baird
said, "O'Neil was a real leader. All the players respected him. He gave
sound advice and seldom raised his voice when a player made a
mistake. He's a credit to baseball and deserves the honor of becoming
the first Negro coach in major league baseball."

could not dine with, or stay at the same hotel as the rest of their team could. While acceptance on the field came rather quickly once integration of the game began, acceptance off of it was far from being fully realized.

Buck O'Neil:

There was no place in Kansas City for them to stay, because when the Yankees came to town, the Yankees would stay downtown at the Muehlebach. But Elston Howard had to stay at the Streets Hotel. That's the same hotel he stayed at when he played with the Monarchs. And I know he felt it. But he knew one thing, one day it would change. And he thought he would be part of that change. And that's what happened. Just like in St. Louis, when Jackie, Joe Black, Campanella, Newcombe, they couldn't stay at the Chase Hotel. They stayed in a black hotel in St. Louis until Jackie started stay-

ing at the hotel. Then they couldn't eat at the hotel until Jackie rebelled, and said "I ain't gonna eat in my room, I'm going down to the dining room and eat." Which kind of scared everybody to death as far as the owners were concerned. But what surprised them all was that the people were delighted to have him there. The customers wanted to get his autograph, and people were saying, "Jackie Robinson's in here," blah, blah, blah, blah. So that changed a lot of things.

And one thing about it is, it wasn't that guy that was coming to the ball park that complained. It was somebody else, and the main thing I think was ownership of the hotel. They thought that they would lose business if the black guys were in the hotel. And so they finally found out. This was one of the reasons actually, that Branch Ricky signed Jackie, was the fact Branch saw the *people that we were putting in the Major League ball parks. And he being a good businessman, he said, "these are some good fans." He figured he would lose a few fans, but he wasn't going to lose many. And the ones that really hated it, would come out to boo. And he had a new clientele. Because we had a built in clientele that we gave to the major leagues. You understand what I mean. Because after Jackie went, the people that had been coming to see us, they wanted to see Jackie, they wanted to see the major leagues. They wanted to see the guy that played in the major leagues.*

The integration of Major League Baseball, proved to be the death of the Negro leagues. By 1955, black baseball was nearly extinct, the talent pools having been depleted by the Major League teams and their minor league clubs, and the once plentiful black fan base now regularly supporting these integrating teams. As Negro league veterans became a desirable commodity to Major League organizations, often a player would make himself even more desirable by subtracting years off of his age. Men in their middle to late thirties, and even forties, suddenly became years younger when presented with this opportunity to play in the big leagues.

Buck O'Neil:

You'd have been a fool to go up there, if the guy wanted to sign you, saying they think you're a ball player, and you going to tell him you're thirty years old and you are thirty, but if you tell him you're twenty-seven, he doesn't know the difference, he'll sign you. You know, thirty, no, you're too old.

The most infamous case of alleged age fixing, was that of Satchel Paige, who was said to be forty-two when he made his Major League debut with the Cleveland Indians, and as old as fifty-nine when he appeared in his final big league season with the Kansas City A's.

Buck O'Neil:

You know actually, you didn't have to bother with Satchel's age. Because everything Satchel did in the major leagues, he was older than anybody there. So there wasn't any need of arguing. He was Satchel Paige. It would have been an attraction if he'd been a hundred. You understand what I mean. Here's a hundred year old man pitching. And this is part of the attraction in the major leagues. This is why. Don't you think Bill Veeck could have found out just how old Satchel was if he wanted to? Yeah, because Satchel was born in Mobile [Alabama]. All he had to do was to go to Mobile. I mean he didn't have to go to Mobile, just call Mobile and find out when

Satchel was born. That Satchel would come up with that thing that his age was in the Bible, and the goat ate the Bible, all that was just a farce. But you could find out the day and everything else. See, if Satchel had been born in some little old hick town out there, where they didn't have the doctors, and the things like that, didn't nothing but mid-wives do it. But in Mobile, if the mid-wife did do it, she's got to keep a record. Man, he was born in the city, he wasn't born in the bushes. But when they'd say, "how old was he?" Didn't nobody know. Didn't nobody know how old Satchel was.

The end of the Negro leagues not only marked the conclusion of one of the richest eras in the history of baseball, it also meant the end of one of the largest black run businesses in the country. The teams of the Negro American and National Leagues, had been a highly profitable venture for their owners.

Integration of the major leagues, quickly turned this into a dying and no longer prosperous situation.

Buck O'Neil:

See what happened when Jackie left, Negro baseball actually had been one of the biggest black businesses in the country. It just wrecked that. The same thing it did to the city black hotels, because we all stayed in the black hotels and ate at the black restaurants, and things like that. But when Jackie went, that opened up a whole lot of other things. And the little man just couldn't compete with the big dollar. So now everybody could stay at the Muehlebach Hotel or the Crown Center. It made a big difference.

But the majority wanted it to happen, because of this fact. The men than owned black baseball, it was just a few that were actually making their living in black base-ball. Just like the major leagues now. No owner is making their living in baseball anymore. See, because the Connie Macks and all that, and the Clark Griffiths, that is gone. Those men, that's where they made the money, the Bill Veecks. They made their money in baseball. Then the billionaire bought baseball and it's a different type of business alto-gether.

CHAPTER 3

Buck O'Neil:

One thing about it is, that we were playing the best that we were allowed to play. Now see, the ones that would have the resentment are the ones that didn't get a chance to play with us, because there wasn't enough room. I could understand him being bitter. If you want to be realistic about it, now if it was a case of somebody I could sue, yeah. But hell, there ain't a damn thing I can do about it, so why be bitter?

The 1955 baseball season was one of the most monumental in the sports history in Kansas City. That year marked the first season for the Kansas City A's, a team that had just relocated from Philadelphia, and the final season for the Monarchs in Kansas City. Each year since Jackie Robinson's debut with the Brooklyn Dodgers in 1947, had been a steady progression of both the players and fans of black baseball to the major leagues. Having the vast majority of black talent under contract with Major League organizations, coupled with the A's arrival, not just to the same city as the Monarchs, but to the same ball park as well, proved to be the final blow to Negro league baseball in Kansas City. Both black and white baseball fans had adopted the newly arrived A's as their team.

At the conclusion of the baseball season Monarch owner, Tom Baird, sold eight of his players to the major leagues, four to the minors, and released his manager Buck O'Neil to became a scout with the Chicago Cubs. O'Neil had a standing offer to join the Cubs from team general manager, Whid Matthews, since former Monarch Ernie Banks went to Chicago in 1953.

The Monarchs meanwhile, were sold to Ted Rasberry, a Michigan businessman, who reformed the team as a Grand Rapids based touring team, that finally dissolved in 1964. While the Kansas City Monarchs' name remained, ultimately nothing else was left that resembled the once great baseball club.

Buck O'Neil:

1955 was the last season; I left in '56. I figured I was going to do something in baseball, because I saw the change. I could see the change coming, and I knew that they were looking for black talent. And at the time, I probably knew more about it than anybody living. So when the Cubs hired me, that's what they hired me for. What they thought was the fact that I knew where to go. Because I'd been there for the Monarchs, you understand. So I knew where to go, and I knew the people that ran the black college ball clubs, because the majority of the time, we'd trained at college campuses. So, I scouted the black colleges all over the country. That's what I was hired for, until they started integration. Then that changed it, and I scouted everybody.

Fifteen seasons after Jackie Robinson integrated baseball, and three following "Pumpsie" Green's debut for the Boston Red Sox, the last Major League team to have a black player, Buck O'Neil became a coach for the Chicago Cubs. It had taken until 1962, that Major League Baseball had hired a non-white coach. It would not be until 1975, that a black man would be named manager of a Major League club when the Cleveland Indians hired Frank Robinson. Maybe not so coincidentally, it had been the Indians under the ownership of Bill Veeck that had made Larry Doby the first black player in the American League twenty-eight years earlier.

Having served as a scout since the 1956 season for the Cubs, Buck O'Neil would again return to the field as a uniformed member of a professional baseball team, something he had not done since managing the Monarchs in their final Kansas City season in 1955. As a short lived experimentation, Chicago instituted the college of coaches, a system in which the job of manager was rotated throughout the season, amongst members of the teams' coaching staff. The fact that the Chicago Cubs lost 103 ball games and finished only ahead of the first year New York Mets in the National League is incidental. The fact that Buck O'Neil was a member of the coaching staff is truly historic.

Buck O'Neil:

I didn't manage. See actually, in that set up we had maybe ten coaches, but just four of them were designated to manage the ball club, and I wasn't one of those. I was just one of the coaches there.

You know actually, the tough thing about that is, at the time when I was the first coach, baseball had to have been seventy-five years old. And now you're just coming up with a black coach. It's as if wasn't nobody before that time qualified to have been a black coach in the major leagues. And I have known so many fellows before me that should have been coaching, managing, general managing, or what not, in Major League Baseball. And I was happy to get the job, but I wasn't happy that I was the first. I think the first should have been fifty years sooner.

Well into the late 1950's and early 1960's, racism was still presented to ball players in various forms, on and off the field. The Cleveland Indians had led the movement of Major League teams to Arizona for spring training to bypass the still rampant segregation of Florida and the deep South. And yet, ironically Arizona presented many of the same racist policies that the teams had sought to escape.

Buck O'Neil:

It was the little things there. They had to be the little things, because we trained in Mesa, the Cubs did. And the black players, Ernie Banks, and say Lou Johnson, George Altman, these guys stayed in different parts of town than the other boys, the white guys. Because they more or less stayed in peoples homes. A lot of them see, because this was then. And the others stayed in black peoples homes. A black man would actually leave his house to them for a time. So this was in a neighborhood that was near the ball park, but it was black. And then, they invited the ball players to play golf on an off day at the country club in Mesa. And well, they didn't want the black guys to play. So Mr. Wrigley said well, nobody would play, see. And some of the guys felt like the black guys knocked them out of a chance to play at the country club. Some of them felt that way about it, see. Because one asked me, you know, why don't you talk to Ernie, because Ernie's going to knock us out of a chance to play at the country club. I said, do you want to play at the country club so bad, that you would actually want me to tell Ernie not to play? I think it kind of shamed him. I could see it kind of shamed him out. But these things did happen. It was a little different in a lot of things in the way they treated ball players.

Major League Baseball had acted quickly on the desegregation of the game, once the color barrier had finally been broken. Talent now became the predominant factor in signing a ball player, eliminating the issue of race that had dominated prior to the 1947 season. By 1962, with baseball fully integrated at the

In 1954, Future Hall of Famer Bob Gibson (left) was just a boy talking to Buck O'Neil. The St. Louis Cardinals signed Gibson in 1957, and he went on to win 276 games in his seventeen years with the major leagues.

Andy Cooper (left) and Oscar Charleston shake hands at Comiskey Park in 1938. The two were the managers for the East-West Game. Cooper was the manager of the Kansas City Monarchs from 1935 until he died in June 1941.

The Kansas City Monarchs' bus.

Satchel Paige. "Once during an exhibition game he [Paige] called the outfielders all in and told them to sit down in the infield. He had everybody sit down behind him. Then he walked three men, on purpose, mind you. Then he struck out the next three," said Ray Dandridge.

The House of David in Benton Harbor, Michigan built a resort colony around its religious activities. They had a number of baseball teams — both black and white.

major league, as well as all minor league levels, the coaching fraternity remained exclusively white, with the exception of Buck O'Neil. It would be an additional thirteen seasons before Frank Robinson would become player-manager for the Cleveland Indians.

Buck O'Neil:

Well we never had a black guy in a position to get the job as a manager in the major leagues, because we had no black managers in minor league baseball. And that is the way the majority of people come to the major leagues, up through the minor league chain. So this is why it took so long. When Jackie went in, and they started hiring black guys, signing them to play major league organized baseball, then if they'd hired some coaches along with it, then you'd have been ready to bring some coaches and managers out.

When Frank Robinson integrated baseball's managerial ranks, he also remained a player, appearing in forty-nine games for the Indians during his first season leading the ball club. Robinson's credentials as a player were stellar, having appeared in five World Series', been named the most valuable player in both the American and National Leagues, and posted statistics that would land him in the Hall of Fame in 1982. Robinson, however, had no managerial or coaching experience of any kind, at any level of baseball, when he was hired for the Cleveland job. The fact that Robinson, who would still play for the Indians, albeit sparingly, was one of baseball's premiere stars and attractions, was not lost on the team's ownership.

Buck O'Neil:

Frank was in the right position at the time to get a job in managing. But during that time, I'm scouting in organized baseball, and as far as my coaching in Major League Base-

*ball, it only lasted two years, be-
cause of the fact that this was Mr.
Wrigley's idea of the college of
coaches. See, and this is why. But if
it hadn't been for the college of
coaches, I wouldn't have been a
coach. But I was one of the scouts,
and I had been working with the ball
club, so I was there, and there it was.*

The National Baseball Hall of Fame and Museum in Cooperstown, New York, has enshrined eleven men for their accomplishments in Negro league baseball, beginning with Satchel Paige in 1971. Since then, Cool Papa Bell, Oscar Charleston, Ray Dandridge, Martin Dihigo, Rube Foster, Josh Gibson, Monte Irvin, Judy Johnson, Buck Leonard, and Pop Lloyd, have received induction, baseball's highest honor. Many players who spent time in the Negro leagues such as Hank Aaron, Willie Mays, and Ernie Banks, but are recognized for their exploits in Major League Baseball, have been inducted into the Hall of Fame as well.

Still, the fact remains that from black baseball's first recognized professional league, the Negro National League in 1920, through Jackie Robinson's Dodger debut in 1947, only eleven participants of this baseball institution have been recognized for enshrinement. When the entire history of Negro league baseball, dating back into the late nineteenth century and extending through the 1960's, is taken into account, the number of Hall of Fame selections appears remarkably small and incomplete.

Buck O'Neil:

Well, I do believe we've got to have as many as ten more that I think should be in the Hall of Fame. Yeah, I'm sure we have that many, and it could be more. But with me, I'm thinking maybe ten more that should get into the Hall of Fame. And one day, I imagine they will get into the Hall of Fame. I thought that we were going to get one more, Leon Day. I thought maybe, and it was close, he just missed out. But I think maybe the way they select the guys, the way they put them in the Hall of Fame, we don't have much of a chance, the way it is handled now. Because, when it was started, it was just the ball player, period. That was all that was going into the Hall of Fame. Then they added the manager, the executives, the umpires, and then the black baseball player. But as I said before, it's hard, the format that they're using now. It's tough, because the baseball player after twenty years, that he was passed over by the writers, now he comes to the veterans committee. Now we're trying to get the guys into the Hall of Fame. The Negro ball player is in competition with the guys that are eligible after twenty years. That's not the baseball player any more. It was at one time, but they put the baseball player in a separate cat-

egory, so we could get someone every year. Because a couple of years, we didn't get anyone, because of the vote. You've got to get seventy-five percent of the vote. So they put the player in a separate category. But, they put the executives, the managers, the umpires, and the Negro league baseball player in one category. So how could I put a Bullet Rogan, Bullet Rogan is eligible for the Hall of Fame, but Bullet Rogan would come up against a Nellie Fox. A Nellie Fox just missed by a few percentage points from the writers. See, he's going to come up against Leo Durocher. He's going to come up against these kind of people. And these kind of people, they've got all the credentials from when they first started in organized baseball. And it's just a few credentials and stats that you got on Bullet Rogan. So it's hard to do. What I'm fighting for is this, put the black ball player in a

*separate category. Just vote on him,
and let them vote on the other people,
the other major leaguers.*

As one of just eighteen members of the Hall of Fame's Veteran's Committee, Buck O'Neil is both influential and instrumental in allowing former Negro league greats to be considered for induction. Ironically, if he were to be elected into the Hall of Fame, his position on the Veteran's Committee would be revoked. Although O'Neil has never been formally considered for enshrinement, his credentials and contributions to both Negro league and Major League Baseball, certainly merit serious consideration. From 1935 to 1955, O'Neil was a member of the Negro leagues, the only exception being two years during World War II, in which he served in the United States Navy. He spent sixteen seasons as first baseman, and then manager for the Kansas City Monarchs, arguably black baseball's greatest team. Following the Monarch's Kansas City departure following the 1955 season, O'Neil became a scout for the Chicago Cubs, discovering many of the club's first black players. In 1962, Buck O'Neil made baseball history, becoming the first black coach in the major leagues. Since returning from military service for the 1946 baseball season, O'Neil has not been away from baseball. He currently is employed by the Kansas City Royals as an advanced scout, a position he has held since 1989. Aside from his aforementioned place on the Hall of Fame's Veteran's Committee, Buck O'Neil also serves as the chairman of the board for the Negro Leagues Baseball Museum in Kansas City, Missouri. His contributions to the sport of baseball on and off of the playing field rank as some of the greatest ever, regardless of recognition, or the lack there of, by baseball's Hall of Fame.

Buck O'Neil:

If I would go into the Hall of Fame, it would be as manager I imagine, if I would go. But there's been so many great managers be-

fore me, see, that just maybe should be in the Hall of Fame, these black guys. Say, Biz Mackey was a great manager. And it took us a long time to get Rube Foster in, who was one of the greatest managers.

Most certainly, Buck O'Neil will be honored in the Negro Leagues Baseball Museum, partially for his contributions to the Museum itself. Upon its completion, the Museum will serve as a shrine to all of the players and contributors to black baseball. Like the baseball Hall of Fame in Cooperstown, New York, the Museum in Kansas City will keep the memory of the game, its teams and players, alive and vibrant.

Buck O'Neil:

Well actually, I always thought, since going to Cooperstown at the Hall of Fame, I thought it would have been a wonderful thing to have a Museum, a Negro Baseball Mu-

seum. And so now we're going to have the Museum right here in Kansas City. Down in the 18th and Vine Street area. We're going to have everything there, a lot of stuff that will be interesting for people to see. And what we're trying to do, we're to actually rejuvenate that area down there, and this is going to help it.

CHAPTER 4

Buck O'Neil:

One thing about it is everybody in this country, you got something mixed up in there. You got some Irish, you got some Spanish, you got some of this, and you got some of that. And I don't know why it's got to be so tainted if a little of it's black. You understand. A guy would say in a minute, I am German something, I'm German-Irish, or German-Jew. Something like that. I don't know why, but if he's black, he's black. You know, nothing but black. Because nobody ever says nothing but black. You black.

It is an arguable point that baseball has lost its standing as the undisputed most popular sport in America, a title it first held from at least the beginning of the twentieth century, and maintained throughout the existence of Negro league baseball and beyond. While it still may be the national pastime, baseball no longer enjoys the huge gap in popularity it once enjoyed over sports such as football and basketball. Two groups from which baseball has clearly lost popularity in recent years are children and blacks. Both participation in baseball, as well as general interest and support of the game, are clearly down, from both of these groups.

Buck O'Neil:

The thing about it, ball players are now coming from the college ranks, see. And the college kids, these guys, the top black athlete's not play-

ing baseball. You look at the College World Series, and you might see out of the eight teams in the College World Series, you might see three black kids. That means the black guy's leaving college to play basketball and football, not baseball. See, at one time, you had these programs, and everybody, the kids wanted to play baseball. What changed this a lot is the popularity of basketball. It's so easy, see all I have to do is put a basket right out there in the middle of the street. And I can put it up there right in the middle of that street, and before the day is over, there's going to be five or six kids out there shooting at that basket. And another thing, I can put it in my backyard for my kids, and he doesn't have to have anybody there. He can do it himself. But with baseball, somebody's got to throw you that damn ball. For you to hit it, somebody's got to throw it to you. For you to catch it, somebody's got to throw it to you. So you can't do nothing by yourself. You got to have somebody. You got to have somebody there, and it's harder to play. Baseball is tough to play, because this sucker's throwing the ball ninety miles an hour. See, and he's not throwing it straight either. And it can hit you.

Major League Baseball does not lack for black stars, yet the fact remains that the crowds and the television audiences for the sport remain overwhelmingly white. This however, is a fairly recent phenomenon in the sport. While support for Major League teams among black fans may have been small prior to integration of the game in 1947, support for Negro league teams by the black community was always high. With the desegregation of the game, and subsequent demise of the Negro leagues, blacks supported both major and minor league baseball in record numbers in the 1950's and 1960's. This is why the relatively recent drop in the black fan base has been so surprising to those in baseball.

Buck O'Neil:

I noticed at our games [Kansas City Royals], not too many black people are coming. And then when Bo Jackson came, it increased. Because, I'm going to take my boy. I want my boy to see Bo. And my boy's going to tell me, I want to go see Bo. It's just like that. And we had Frank White all the time. But you got a magnet there. It's somebody that everybody wants to see. And one thing about it is, we're getting a lot of athletes now, that played other sports, that's coming into baseball now. And I think Bo Jackson's had a lot to do with that. Yeah, because there's so many kids that are good basketball players. But they don't go to the NBA. Good basketball players don't go to the NBA. See, you've got to be better than good. So this is the same thing, supply is greater than the demand. It might start to change, just like the Deion Sanders, the Bo Jacksons, when these top athletes in some other sport start playing. Because the money's right there for them.

As a baseball scout, Buck O'Neil understands first hand about the matriculation of top black athletes to basketball and football, and away from baseball. College programs in these sports are drawing from those athletes who, a generation earlier, would have most likely opted to play baseball. And certainly, college baseball remains a minor sport at most colleges and universities, while football and basketball, generate the vast majority of revenue, publicity, and prestige.

Buck O'Neil:

Actually, a recruiter from Missouri [University] *would come in*

Buck O'Neil (standing, far right) in the Monarchs' dugout. Seated on his right is Frank Duncan whose son, Frank, was a Monarch catcher and manager for many years.

In 1948, Satchel Paige's All-Stars traveled all over the country in this airplane when they played a series of games against Bob Feller's All-Stars. Pictured, left to right, Hilton Smith, Howard Easterling, Barney Brown, Sam Jethroe, Gentry Jessup, Hank Thompson, Max Manning, Othello Renfroe, William (Dizzy) Dismukes, Rufus Lewis, Gene Benson, Buck O'Neil, Frank Duncan, Artie Wilson and Quincy Trouppe. In the doorway are a valet and Paige.

At the start of the 1926 season, the Monarchs became the first team to travel exclusively by bus. Owner J. L. Wilkinson, seeking a more economical mode of transportation than trains, bought an eighteen-seater that had specially constructed cushions with reclining seats.

Left to right, John (Buck) O'Neil, Frank Duncan, James (Jew Baby) Floyd, Wilber (Bullet) Rogan. All four enjoyed long careers with the Monarch organization. O'Neil joined the team in 1938 and remained until it was sold in 1955. Duncan came to the Monarchs in 1922 and retired in 1947. Floyd was the team's trainer from 1920 to 1949. Rogan, an original Monarch, signed with the club in 1920 and retired at age forty-nine in 1938.

ube Foster, the Father of the Negro Leagues. Player, manager, and founder of the Negro ational League, the first nationally recognized black league. Shown with his wife, Sarah.

Left to right, Buck O'Neil, _______ Vaughn, Robert Motley, Frank Duncan and Oscar Charleston before a game in 1949.

here and recruit a guy for basket-ball, and this guy could also play baseball. Just say if he comes in here to get him, and I'd go out there and try to get him, I can't compete with the University of Missouri. Because he's coming from here to go play big league college basketball. Coming from here, he ain't going to play big league baseball. He's got to go some-place else before he gets there. So, he's got a selling point that I don't have. So, actually, there's no way for me to compete with this boy going to Missouri to play basketball, or to Notre Dame to play football. But he's a good baseball player. How in the hell am I going to compete with Notre Dame? Because the coach is going to come in here, and talk to his momma, and talk to his poppa. This boy's going to Notre Dame.

So actually, what he's going to do, this top athlete, he's going into bas-ketball. He's going into football. And see, what they don't do, they don't take mediocre black kids. See, this is what's happening. Any black kid that goes to a white school to play basketball, he's one of the best. Whereas a white kid doesn't have to be one of the best. They see the potential he might become. He's got a chance to become one of the best. But the black kid that they go out there and get, he's top dog. He can play. This is why they are so good, they're leaving so many back here. You see, they're actually picking the cream of the crop. They go get him, and put him there. So he can actually play, he's a top athlete. Now, that's basketball, football. And then it's a short way there, right out of college. Boom, you're a star. See, right out of college, you can catch a football, you're right there. But you come with me, I've got to send you to backwater baseball, or some other place.

As a player and then manager for the Kansas City Monarchs, Buck O'Neil was a role model in his community, to all of his fans. It was a part of being a baseball player, and remains as such in today's game. A top athlete possesses the ability to cross all social and ethnic lines, and attract fans based upon his or her on-field credentials. This remains as true in sports now, as it did when people, white and black, would come out to see O'Neil and the Kansas City Monarchs play.

Buck O'Neil:

If you put nine black guys on a ball club that can win a championship, ain't nobody going to say a damn thing. And you know the amazing thing about sports, a kid, he doesn't give a damn what color you are. This is a kid. See, a kid will come up in a minute and say, "well who do you like in that ball game? Well I like Bo Jackson." Doesn't matter what he is. You understand what

I mean. This is what a kid will say. Now a guy eighteen might not say it. He might feel it, and won't say it. Because he's afraid what his peers will say. And a black kid is supposed to like Bo Jackson, and he might like George Brett. But he's scared to say it. You know, he's eighteen years old now, sixteen, seventeen, eighteen years old. But it didn't matter to him when he was eight or nine years old. The one thing he likes, if he takes a fancy to him, he doesn't care about color. And actually, if we would just let the kids, if we could just think like them all the way through, it would be a beautiful world. See, but after you get a little older, that little peer pressure starts coming in, and now you change your way of thinking.

Negro league baseball is currently in a Renaissance period, fueled by a renewed interest in the players and teams that often toiled in relative obscurity next to their Major League counterparts, yet rose to heights of super-stardom in the nation's black communities. Now, white and black baseball fans alike, are searching out the history and essence of this once forgotten brand of baseball. For Buck O'Neil, fame is presently in the form of a second coming, as he once again stands as one of the most recognizable and sought out sports figures in Kansas City. He has also become one of the unofficial spokesmen and keepers of the flame for black baseball, always remaining friendly and accessible to all who are interested in learning about the history of his league, the Negro leagues.

Buck O'Neil:

Things are happening now that never happened before. Because right now, the Monarchs, we're on television two or three times a year. And these people are starting to recognize us. We went to the movies last night, and we got out of the movie, and my wife went to buy some popcorn. And I saw a lady and a man that kept looking at me, and I said, well I must know them, see, and I don't want them to think I ignored them or something like that. I smiled and walked over toward them. And they said, "You're that old baseball player." And I said, yes, I am. They said, "Well yeah, I saw you on television," and so on, and these things. You see, this is actually coming more now than ever before. Now, twenty years ago, nobody would have been here. Because, you know what I mean, he didn't care nothing about knowing about it. But right now, there has been an awakening on, as far as guys like me.

APPENDIX

I first met Buck O'Neil when I was twenty years old, working in my first season as a radio reporter in Kansas City covering the Royals. He was standing around the batting cage before the game, looking as though he could still get in there and take some cuts. His dress was exquisite, his clothes as stylish as any modern ball player would wear. His body looked strong, definitely that of an athlete. I would later learn that he still weighs the same as he did when playing first base for the Monarchs. His face looked kind, and far, far younger than that of a man in his late seventies. And although I had idolized this man for many years from afar, had long known of his greatness and triumphs, I was scared as hell to approach him. After all, here was Buck O'Neil, my idol, my hero, standing not five feet from me. What would I say? Why would he want to meet me? Sensing an opportunity of infinite importance however, I summoned up the courage, and put forth a very meager "excuse me, Mr. O'Neil." To my sheer delight, but maybe not necessarily to my surprise, Buck O'Neil was as friendly a man as I had ever met, anywhere. I sensed that he genuinely felt my enthusiasm and feeling of awe, and thus enjoyed talking with me all the more.

In the four years since that first meeting, I have come to know not only Buck O'Neil the baseball legend, but Buck O'Neil the man. He always has a kind word for me, and time to talk when I see him at the ball park. He always makes me feel as though our conversations mean something to him as well.

His life is something that I can barely fathom, even after writing this book, and having spent hours talking with him. It is a life that will never be led by anyone again. He is a testament to an era that has long since vanished, never to return. He remains a man of elegance and grace, of warmth and caring. He is sheer baseball history, and yet when I see him at the ball park, he looks perfectly placed in the modern game.

Before I met Buck O'Neil, when I only knew of this man through his accomplishments and exploits in the game of baseball, I knew that he was someone very special. Now, four years after finally meeting him, I can call Buck O'Neil my friend. And as always, I can still call him my hero.

May, 1994
Kansas City

BIBLIOGRAPHY

Bruce, Janet. *The Kansas City Monarchs: Champions of Black Baseball.* University Press of Kansas, 1985.

Dixon, Phil with Hannigan, Patrick J. *The Negro Baseball Leagues: A Photographic History.* Amereon House, 1992.

Etkin, Jack. *Innings Ago.* Normandy Square Publications, 1987.

Holway, John B. *Black Diamonds.* Stadium Books, 1991.

Okrent, Daniel and Wulf, Steve. *Baseball Anecdotes.* Oxford University Press, 1989.

Reichler, Joseph L., editor. *The Baseball Encyclopedia*. MacMillan Publishing Company, 1992.

Reidenbaugh, Lowell. *Take Me Out to the Ball Park*. The Sporting News, 1985.

Rogosin, Donn. *Invisible Men: Life in Baseball's Negro leagues*. Atheneum, 1987.

Tygiel, Jules. *Baseball's Great Experiment: Jackie Robinson and His Legacy*. Vintage Books, 1983.

BUCK O'NEIL CHRONOLOGY

1911   John Jordan "Buck" O'Neil is born in Carabelle, Florida on November 13.

1924   O'Neil moves with his family to Sarasota, Florida. It is in Sarasota, the spring training home of the New York Giants, that O'Neil first watches professional baseball.

1928   O'Neil begins attending Edward Waters College in Jacksonville, Florida, a small African Methodist Episcopal school. O'Neil completes four years of high school and two years of college, playing all six years on the baseball team.

1934   O'Neil makes his debut as a professional baseball player, with the Miami Giants. The Giants barnstorm along the east coast, a tour that includes O'Neil's first trip to New York City and Harlem. It is with the team that O'Neil receives his nickname "Buck," from one of the Miami Giants' two owners, Buck O'Neal. The team returns to Miami, playing throughout the winter.

1935   O'Neil returns for his second season with the Miami Giants, now known as the New York Tigers. The team plays in the first National Baseball Congress tournament in Wichita, Kansas. At the tournament's end, O'Neil watches the Kansas City Monarchs for the first time, as they play the NBC championship team from Bismarck, North Dakota, a team that features Satchel Paige.

1936   O'Neil switches clubs, joining the Acme Giants based in Shreveport, Louisiana. O'Neil had been offered a contract by the club's owner, Winfield Welch, who had seen him play the season before. Welch is sponsored by J. L. Wilkinson, owner of the Kansas City Monarchs, thus operating the Acme Giants as a farm team. With the Acme Giants, O'Neil barnstorms from Shreveport to western Canada.

1937   O'Neil returns to the Acme Giants for spring training, who are sharing their camp in Shreveport with the Kansas City Monarchs. The Monarchs sign O'Neil, but loan him to the Memphis Red Sox so that he may receive more playing time. After a brief stint with the Red Sox, O'Neil jumps clubs to the Zulu Cannibal Giants, a team that features showmanship, trickery, and ball players in straw skirts.

1938   O'Neil becomes a member of the Kansas City Monarchs, the team with which he is most prominently associated, and with whom he will remain until their departure from Kansas City after the 1955 season. As a first baseman and right fielder, O'Neil makes $100 a month for the Negro American League club.

1939   O'Neil bats a recorded .257 with two home runs against Negro American League competition. The Kansas City Monarchs win the first half of the season, and then defeat the St. Louis Stars three games to two in a post season series, for the Negro American League championship.

1940   O'Neil has one of his best seasons as a professional batting .364 in league play, as the Monarchs capture both the first and second half Negro American League titles.

1941   O'Neil faces Bob Feller in a game featuring stars from the Negro Leagues and Major League Baseball, the first of many encounters. Although a full season with the Kansas City Monarchs is played, there are no published standings for the Negro American League.

1942   O'Neil plays on perhaps the greatest Kansas City Monarchs team ever, which sweeps the Homestead Grays four games to none, claiming the first Negro League World Series contested between the Negro American and National Leagues. O'Neil also appears in his first of eight East-West Negro League All-Star Games, and faces the Dizzy Dean All-Stars, comprised of players from Major League Baseball. The championship Monarchs feature O'Neil as well as Satchel Paige, Hilton Smith, Connie Johnson, Newt Allen, and Ted Strong.

1943   O'Neil makes his second consecutive East-West Negro League All-Star

Game appearance, before being inducted into the United States Navy in August. World War II depletes the rosters of Negro League teams as dramatically as it does the Major League teams. Both brands of baseball see their product drastically altered and diminished during Word War II.

1944-45   O'Neil serves as a U.S. Navy CB (construction battalion) primarily in Subic Bay, Philippines. With many of their starters in military service, the Kansas City Monarchs struggle on the field.

1946   O'Neil returns to the Kansas City Monarchs after a two season absence, hitting a league leading .350. With their roster fully restored, the Monarchs again reach the Negro League World Series, losing to the Newark Eagles four games to three. O'Neil then plays for the Satchel

Paige All-Stars, touring the country with the Bob Feller All-Stars, and then joins Almendares in the multi-racial Cuban winter league.

1947   O'Neil follows his batting title with a .358 average for the Kansas City Monarchs, and returns to Almendares for a second season of Cuban winter baseball. It is a member of the 1945 Monarchs, however, that alters the sport forever, when Jackie Robinson makes his debut with the Brooklyn Dodgers, thus breaking Major League Baseball's color barrier.

1948   O'Neil becomes manager of the Kansas City Monarchs after playing eight seasons for the ball club. Replacing Frank Duncan who had managed the Monarchs since 1943, O'Neil serves as player/manager through the 1955 season. The promotion of O'Neil to manager is brought about when Tom Baird purchases the controlling interest in the team from J. L. Wilkinson prior to the start of the season. The O'Neil led Monarchs claim the second half of the Negro American League season, then lose to the Birmingham Black Barons four games to three in a playoff for the league championship.

1949   O'Neil appears in his third East-West Negro League All-Star game, and registers a .330 average in Negro American League play. The Monarchs are victorious in the first half of the season, but refuse to meet the second half champion Chicago American Giants for the Negro American League title due to the loss of many of their top players to major and minor league clubs.

1950   O'Neil manages the Kansas City Monarchs to both the first and second half titles, thus automatically giving the club the Negro American

League championship. The Monarchs start Elston Howard in left field and rookie Ernie Banks at shortstop.

1951   O'Neil appears in his fourth East-West Negro League All-Star game, his first as a manager for the West Squad. O'Neil still remains active as a player, for both the Monarchs and Obregon in the Mexican winter league.

1952   O'Neil again serves as manager in the East-West Negro League All-Star game, one of the six Kansas City Monarch representatives. Desperate for players due to the top black baseball talent now in the Major Leagues, and to the Negro leagues, the Monarchs offer a contract to 15 year old Bob Gibson, who declines.

1953   O'Neil bats .476 in limited action for the Kansas City Monarchs, now just one of four teams remaining in the

Negro American League. The Monarchs lose Ernie Banks, who signs with the Chicago Cubs. Banks is the last great player to be produced by the Negro Leagues. O'Neil again serves as manager in the East-West Negro League All-Star game.

1954   O'Neil again remains effective as a part-time player batting .338 for the Kansas City Monarchs. As manager in the East-West Negro League All-Star game, O'Neil is before a crowd of barely 10,000, down from almost 50,000 a decade earlier.

1955   O'Neil manages and plays in his final season for the Kansas City Monarchs, a team which he joined as a player in 1938. O'Neil also manages in his final East-West Negro League all-star game, his eighth appearance in the contest. The Philadelphia A's have relocated to Kansas City for the start of the season, claming almost all baseball interest in the city. The Monarchs play only two games in their home town, based on their mounting financial losses and inability to attract fans. After the season, Tom Baird sells the Monarchs name, uniforms, and equipment to Ted Rasberry, who relocates the team to Grand Rapids, Michigan. O'Neil is released from his Monarchs' contract and signs with the Chicago Cubs as a scout.

1956-88 O'Neil serves as a scout for the Chicago Cubs, first assigned to locate black talent. From scouting black colleges, O'Neil discovers and signs Lou Brock in 1960. In 1962, O'Neil is named to the Cubs coaching staff, becoming the first black coach in Major League history. Chosen to be a coach in the Major League All-Star Game, O'Neil wears a Kansas City Monarch uniform. In 1981 O'Neil is appointed to the National Baseball

Hall of Fame's Veterans Committee, while continuing to serve as a scout for the Cubs.

1989-present

O'Neil joins the Kansas City Royals as a scout, once again affiliated with baseball in the city that he first represented in 1938. In 1991, O'Neil is named as Chairman of the Board for the Negro Leagues Baseball Museum, headquartered in Kansas City, Missouri. In his role as chairman, O'Neil is instrumental in the Museum's Kansas City opening in the summer of 1994. Also in 1994, O'Neil is prominently featured in Ken Burns' documentary film "Baseball." Buck O'Neil remains a resident of Kansas City, living with his wife, Ora, in a house he purchased while playing with the Monarchs. He continues as a scout for the Kansas City Royals, working every home game at Kauffman Stadium.

INDEX